Basics

A Trio of Sauces
Easy Onion Gravy

Serves 4 | 20 minutes
A classic, simple gravy that works with most dishes.

- 2 medium red or white onions
- 1 large sprig of fresh rosemary or ½ tsp dried
- 350ml/1½ cups vegan stock
- 2 tbsp soya sauce
- 1 level tsp dark brown sugar
- Salt (add last as the stock may be salty) and black pepper

Optional extras
- A handful of dried mushrooms soaked in the stock then blended
- For a thicker gravy, mix in 1 tbsp arrowroot with the soya sauce and a splash of water to make a paste. Add this to the gravy and cook in for a few minutes

1 Peel the onions and cut into thin wedges or blitz in a food processor.
2 Heat the oil in the saucepan and sauté the onions over a gentle heat. Stir occasionally for about 10 minutes until they are soft and starting to caramelise.
3 Add the rosemary, stock, soya sauce and brown sugar. Add any optional extras now.
4 Simmer for 5-7 minutes, adjusting seasoning if necessary. Serve hot.

All kitted out
- Chopping board and knife • Measuring jug or cups
- Measuring spoons • Saucepan and cooking spoon
- Stick blender or similar

If you're in a hurry, use ready-made vegan gravy such as Marigold, Bisto Onion or Classic (red tub) or Sainsbury's. Free & Easy sell a free-from, liquid gravy in a pouch. Other brands may be suitable but check they are vegan.

Mushroom, Miso & Mustard Sauce

Serves 2-4 (makes approx 500ml/2 cups) | 10-15 minutes

This is delicious and works with many dishes from stir-fries to sausages, burgers to grains! It also freezes well, so feel free to make a double batch and stash half for a busy day.

Base mix
- 2 tsp oil
- 1 bunch spring onions, trimmed and chopped roughly
- 150g/2 cups mushrooms, any type, roughly chopped
- 2 cloves garlic, peeled and quartered OR 1 tsp garlic paste

Everything else
- 300ml/1¼ cups water
- 60ml/¼ cup dry white wine
- 2 tbsp arrowroot
- 2 tbsp medium miso (the reddish-brown type)
- 3 tbsp nutritional yeast
- 1 tsp Dijon mustard (use English if you don't have Dijon)
- Black pepper to taste

1 In the saucepan, heat the oil and sauté the onion, mushrooms and garlic until softened – about 3 minutes. Stir regularly so the garlic doesn't catch and burn and add a splash of water if necessary.

2 Mix the arrowroot with the wine to make a smooth paste. Add this and everything else to the mushroom mixture. Bring to the boil and simmer for 5-6 minutes to let the arrowroot and wine cook in a little. Stir regularly to avoid lumps.

3 Blend in short blasts to achieve the texture you prefer. Taste, adjust seasoning if necessary and serve hot.

All kitted out
- Chopping board and knife • Measuring spoons
- Scales or measuring cups • Medium saucepan
- Cooking spoon • Stick blender or similar

Tahini Orange Sauce

Serves 2-3 | 5 minutes

This is deliciously simple. It can be used cold, as a dressing or warmed gently to accompany grain or vegetable dishes such as Buddha bowls and stir-fries.

- ½ tsp orange zest
- 120ml/½ cup orange juice
- 120ml/½ cup tahini
- 1 tbsp soya sauce
- 1 tsp agave syrup
- ¼ tsp crushed garlic or paste
- A splash or two of water if the sauce is too thick

1 Mix the tahini in the bowl or saucepan with the orange juice and zest. Whisk until smooth.
2 Add everything else. Taste and adjust flavouring if desired, eg more salt, soya sauce or orange juice. Serve as it is or warm gently – don't boil as it will make the sauce too thick.

All kitted out
- Bowl • Small spatula • Small saucepan for warmed version • Measuring jug or cups • Measuring spoons
- Small whisk or fork • Zester or grater

Sage Seitan Sausages

Makes 6-8 sausages | 40-45 minutes, 30 of which is steaming time

This is a simple and very tasty recipe. Vital gluten flour can be found in good health food shops or online (not to be confused with gluten-free flour!). It's worth shopping around because prices vary. The sausages freeze well so it's worth making a double batch.

- 2 tsp dried sage
- ½ tsp salt
- 1 tsp onion powder
- 1 tsp garlic powder
- 60g/½ cup vital wheat gluten flour
- 2 tbsp chickpea flour (also called besan or gram flour)
- 2 tsp oil
- 1 tbsp tomato sauce or purée
- 100-120ml/½ cup water – add the minimum and then a splash more if mixture is too dry

Ready-made chunks or slices
- Granovita Mock Duck – Holland & Barrett, health food shops, Ocado.
- Biona, Yakso or Lima brands (basic seitan that's also organic) – health food shops.
- Companion Brand or Mong Lee Shang brands are sold mainly in East Asian supermarkets. Companion Brand sells a wide range of vegan products, eg mock duck, mock chicken, vegetarian tuna. www.companionfoods.com.

1 Bring the steamer water to simmer.
2 Mix everything together in the bowl and knead for 2-3 minutes to ensure all the flavours become integrated with the dough. The dough is sticky, so while you can knead it with bare hands, feel free to wear disposable gloves or use a dough hook attachment if you have one.
3 Split the dough up into roughly even sections – eight or six pieces. Shape into sausages.
4 Double wrap each sausage using two pieces of foil OR one piece of baking paper and one of foil. Wrap each layer up separately – seal the seams of each layer, by pinching them, to prevent water leaking in.
5 Place in one or two tiers of a steamer and steam for 30 minutes, turning the sausages once.
6 Once cooked remove from the steamer and let them cool before removing their wrappings. Let them cool down on a rack before using. They will keep in the fridge for 2-3 days or can be frozen for another time.
7 To cook, fry up in a little oil until browned on the outside and hot in the middle.

All kitted out
- Mixing bowl • Scales or measuring cups
- Measuring spoons • Steamer with at least two tiers
- Tinfoil • Mixing spoon • Optional dough hook (on an electric mixer) or disposable gloves

Seitan originates from 6th century China and is healthy, high in protein, inherently low in fat and very tasty when flavoured. However, it is unsuitable for those with coeliac disease or a medically diagnosed wheat/gluten intolerance. It is used to create a variety of vegan meats. As you'll see from this recipe, it is simple, cheap and easy to make at home. There are also some great YouTube videos if you prefer to see a demonstration first. Or buy it ready-made – we've done the research for you!

All kitted out
• Measuring scales or cups • Measuring spoons • Mixing bowl and sieve • Balloon whisk or mixing spoon • Small bowl for flax 'egg' • Jug or bowl • Frying pan • 'Fish' slice/turner • Oven tray

Breakfasts

Breakfast Pancakes

Serves 4 | 30 minutes
This recipe makes thick, fluffy, American-style stacking-style pancakes – very good!

- Flax egg: 1 tbsp flax meal (ground flax/linseed) + 3 tbsp water

Dry ingredients
- 150g/1 cup plain flour
- 1 tsp baking powder
- ¼ tsp bicarbonate of soda
- ¼ tsp salt

Vegan buttermilk
- 240-250ml/1 cup plant milk, eg soya or almond
- 1 tsp cider vinegar

Oil
- 1 tbsp plain vegetable oil or melted coconut oil

To serve
- Berries, banana slices, syrup – date, maple or agave
- Coconut cream, peanut butter, chocolate chips or sauce also work well
- For a savoury alternative, serve with vegan rashers, sausages or similar

1 To make the flax 'egg', mix the flax meal with the water in a small bowl and set aside.
2 Pre-heat the oven and set it to a medium-low heat to keep the cooked pancakes warm – 150-160°C/300-320°F/Gas Mark 2-3.
3 Sieve the dry ingredients into a bowl and mix together.
4 In a bowl or jug, mix the plant milk and cider vinegar together to make the vegan buttermilk.
5 Prepare and measure whichever type of oil you are using and add to the buttermilk mixture. If using coconut oil, remove the metal lid from the jar and soften the oil in the microwave. Add it to the buttermilk mixture, whisking in quickly.
6 Make a hole in the middle of the dry ingredients and gently stir in the buttermilk mixture. Mix well but gently, so the pancakes don't become tough. This makes a thick mixture.
7 Heat a non-stick frying pan. Test if it is hot enough by splashing a small drop of water in it – it should spit. Use oil spray or brush vegetable oil over the bottom of the pan.
8 Use a quarter measuring cup or approx 4 tablespoons to make each small pancake.
9 Spoon the batter into the pan and let the pancakes cook for a minute or two until large bubbles form on the top (this means the first side has cooked). Reduce the heat a little if they brown too quickly. Flip then cook for another minute or so. The pancakes will be very fluffy and slightly moist in the middle.
10 Place each pancake onto the oven tray and keep warm while you finish the rest of the batch. Serve with the options of your choice.

Golden Turmeric Milk

Serves 1 | 5 minutes

Turmeric contains anti-inflammatory properties and antioxidants so it's good to include it in your diet as much as possible. This recipe is a delicious way to do it!

- 250ml/1 cup plant milk
- 1cm root turmeric
- Pinch black pepper
- 1-2 Medjool dates, pitted

1 Blend all ingredients together.
2 Sieve the mixture through a nut milk bag, muslin or tights.
3 Serve cold or warm gently on a low-medium heat without boiling.

Optional: sprinkle with cinnamon.

All kitted out
- Blender • Nut milk bag, muslin cloth or (clean) pair of tights • Small knife • Small saucepan (if heating)

Quick Silken Tofu Scramble

Serves 1-2 | 5-10 minutes
Our favourite scramble recipe. Quick, tasty and really easy to make!

- 1 tsp vegetable oil
- 1 clove garlic (peeled and crushed) OR ½ -1 tsp garlic purée
- 175g firm silken tofu (approximately ½ packet long life) OR same quantity of firm tofu, drained and pressed
- 1 tsp tahini
- 1 tbsp soya sauce
- 1 tbsp nutritional yeast flakes
- ½ tsp turmeric

Optional extras: sliced avocado, sliced tomato, chopped peppers or chilli, rocket or kale.

1 Gently fry the garlic in the oil for about 30 seconds until lightly golden. Don't let it burn.
2 Add all the other ingredients and mix together gently. Try not to break up the tofu too much but make sure it is well stirred.
3 Heat through for approximately 3-5 minutes and serve immediately. It will keep in the fridge for a couple of days.

Silken tofu, as its name suggests, is silky smooth, so its consistency makes it very versatile in dips and desserts also. Buy it in long-life packs or fresh (eg Taifun or East Asian grocers). The best long-life brands for scramble are Morinaga, Morinu, Blue Dragon and Yukata and you'll find one of these brands in most large supermarkets as well as health food or East Asian shops. We particularly like the extra-firm variety.

All kitted out
- Small knife • Garlic crusher • Medium saucepan
- Scissors • Measuring spoons • Cooking spoon

Vegan French Toast

Serves 2-4 | 20 minutes

- Half a pack of firm silken tofu (approximately 175g/6oz)
- 120ml/4fl oz soya or other unsweetened plant milk, eg almond
- 1 tbsp vegetable oil
- 1 tbsp nutritional yeast flakes (Marigold's Engevita brand, sold in health food stores or good delis)
- Salt and black pepper. For a more 'eggy' taste use Himalayan black salt
- 4-6 slices of bread, medium thick – we prefer good quality white, but granary or wholemeal would also work well. The number of slices you can make depends on whether the bread is from a large or small loaf
- Oil spray or oil to fry

1 Blend the tofu until almost smooth.
2 Add the plant milk, yeast flakes, salt and pepper and whizz again.
3 Heat a non-stick frying pan until hot. Drizzle a little oil in the pan or spray with a couple of squirts of oil spray.
4 Depending on the size of your frying pan, coat 1-2 slices of bread in the mixture and place in the pan.
5 Cook for several minutes on each side until crispy and golden brown – make sure the bread isn't soggy.
6 Repeat the process until the mixture is used up. Serve hot.

All kitted out
- Blender • Frying pan • Measuring spoons
- Measuring jug • Wide bowl • 'Fish' slice/turner

Lunches, light meals & sides

Souperday!
Living Thai Soup

Serves 1 | 5-10 minutes

- ½ large mug of boiling water
- ¾ medium carrot, peeled
- ¼ red pepper
- ½ apple
- 1cm ginger
- 1cm red chilli (deseeded)
- Couple of sprigs coriander or ¼ flat teaspoon of dried coriander
- Splash of plant milk
- 1 tsp bouillon powder (e.g. Marigold vegan)

1 Place all ingredients into the blender, pouring on the boiling water last, and blend until smooth.
2 Serve immediately.

All kitted out
- Chopping board • Small knife • Large mug • Blender
- Kettle

Pistou Soup

Serves 4-6 | 40-50 minutes

This hearty soup is packed with lovely deep flavours and makes a satisfying lunch or light supper. Pistou is the French version of pesto and is used as a garnish on the soup.

Soup

- 2 tbsp olive oil
- 1 large red onion, diced
- 2 carrots, diced
- 4 cloves garlic, crushed OR 2 tsp paste
- 3 sprigs fresh thyme or ½ tsp dried
- 3 bay leaves
- 4 tbsp tomato purée
- 2L/8 cups strong vegan stock
- Pinch of sugar or tiny drizzle of agave
- 100g/½ cup orzo (small, rice-shaped pasta. Use the same amount of white rice if you're gluten-free)
- 200g/1⅓ cups French beans – frozen work well
- 2 courgettes, diced
- 200g/1⅓ cups frozen peas
- 1 tin white beans, rinsed and drained, eg haricot or cannellini
- Salt and freshly ground pepper to taste

Pistou

- 1 large bunch of basil – use Thai basil or regular
- 1 heaped tbsp of lemon grass paste or 1 stalk, chopped roughly
- ½ a red chilli, deseeded and roughly chopped
- 2-3 tbsp plain vegetable oil
- A splash of water if necessary

1 Prepare the vegetables and get everything ready to go.
2 In a large saucepan, heat the oil and lightly fry the onion and garlic for a couple of minutes. Add the carrots and fry for another minute. Add the thyme, bay leaves, stock, tomato purée and sugar/agave.
3 Bring to the boil and simmer for about 5 minutes.
4 Meanwhile, make the pistou by blending the ingredients to a paste in a food processor. Using a rubber spatula, scrape it out into an attractive bowl and set aside.
5 Add the orzo/rice, courgettes, French beans and peas to the soup. Cook on a medium heat according to the pasta packet instructions until the orzo and vegetables are just cooked – *al dente*. Add the white beans and heat through. (The beans can be blended with a few tablespoons of the soup liquid if you prefer.)
6 Taste and season with salt and black pepper as necessary. Remove the bay leaves and sprigs of thyme if using.
7 Serve the hot soup in bowls with a dollop of pistou on top.

All kitted out

- Chopping board and knife • Scales or measuring cups • Measuring spoons • Large saucepan and cooking spoon • Jug for stock • Tin opener • Colander
- Food processor or small blender

Sandwiches
Smashed Chickpea Salad Sandwich

Makes at least four sandwiches | 5-10 minutes

This lovely, complex-tasting filling is easy and cheap to make, especially if you have most of the ingredients already.

- 1 tin chickpeas, drained and rinsed (save the bean water – aquafaba – as an egg replacer in baking, mayonnaise etc)
- 4-5 finely chopped gherkins OR 2 large gherkins. Start small and add more to taste if you wish
- 4 spring onions, finely chopped
- 2-3 tbsp vegan mayonnaise thinned down with a tablespoon or two of unsweetened plant milk
- 1-2 tsp Dijon mustard, according to taste
- 1½ tsp cider vinegar (optional – this depends on the tartness of your mayo)
- Salt to taste
- 2-3 tbsp fresh chopped dill or parsley
- 1 tsp turmeric
- Lots of fresh black pepper
- Good quality bread of your choice

Optional extras – some or all of these
- Alfalfa or other small sprouts
- Grated carrot
- Dark green leaves, e.g. rocket or watercress
- Tomato, thinly sliced
- Avocado, mashed or sliced

1 Mash the chickpeas with a potato masher – the mixture should be mostly mashed but keep some texture.
2 Add the rest of the ingredients and mix well.
3 Taste and adjust seasoning if necessary.
4 Create your sandwich with the bread and other fillings of your choosing.
5 The filling will last for 2-3 days in an airtight container in the fridge.

All kitted out
- Chopping board and knife • Tin opener
- Potato masher • Mixing spoon • Medium bowl
- Measuring spoons

Tempeh Rasher & Avocado Sandwich

Serves 1+ | 3 minutes

Another quick, tasty sarnie. You'll find tempeh rashers in Holland & Barrett and other health food shops.

- Nice bread of your choice
- Vegan margarine if desired (but the avocado is creamy and rich)
- Mustard and/or vegan mayo
- Pre-cooked tempeh slices, any flavour you like
- Avocado, mashed or sliced
- Lime juice
- Salt and black pepper

1 If using margarine, spread it on both sides of the bread.
2 Mash the avocado with a fork and spread it on one side of the bread.
3 Sprinkle with salt, pepper and lime juice.
4 Place the tempeh rashers on the top and then place second piece of bread on top. Press down firmly and slice in half.
5 Eat or wrap it up for later.

All kitted out
• Sharp knife • Fork • Scissors • Spatula or table knife

Lunches
Carrot, Beetroot & Cumin Burgers

Makes 8-10 burgers | 1 hour or less
We've given double quantities for this recipe because they are so good you'll probably want to freeze them! Alternatively, halve or quarter the amounts.

- 2 medium onions (diced)
- 3 cloves garlic (crushed)
- 500g/10 cups coarsely grated mixed carrot and beetroot grated (using the second biggest holes of the grater)
- 50g/1 cup fresh coriander, chopped
- 2 tsp toasted and ground cumin seeds
- 2 tsp paprika powder
- 2 tins chickpeas, drained and ground roughly in food processor (or crushed with potato masher)
- 100g ground flax
- Salt (enough to create good, strong flavour before they are cooked)

1 Pre-heat oven to 200°C/400°F/Gas Mark 6.
2 Fry the onion until lightly browned on a medium heat. Add the garlic and fry for a minute or two.
3 Mix all ingredients together in a large mixing bowl until fully combined but not completely smooth (this is best done using your hands).
4 Shape the mixture into ten balls and then flatten and shape into burgers (if you are freezing any of the burgers, put them in the freezer at this stage).
5 Place on a lined baking tray and heat in the oven for around 30 minutes or until lightly browned.

All kitted out
- Knife • Chopping board • Measuring spoons
- Frying pan • Spatula • Food processor or potato masher • Large mixing bowl • Baking tray
- Baking paper

Warm Lentil & Roasted Squash Salad

Serves 4 | 1 hour or less

- 2 tbsp olive oil
- 300g dried French, green or brown lentils
- 600ml water
- 1 butternut squash (peeled and chopped into small, bite-sized pieces)
- 1 tsp paprika
- Salt and black pepper (to taste)
- Rocket or other salad leaves
- Toasted seeds
- Greek-style vegan cheese (optional)
- Marinated tofu (optional… see our recipe on page 33)

French dressing
- ¼ clove garlic
- 2 tbsp cider vinegar
- 6 tbsp extra virgin olive oil
- 1 tsp Dijon mustard
- 1 tsp vegan syrup (eg agave or maple syrup)

1 Pre-heat the oven to 200°C/400°F/Gas Mark 6.
2 Place the peeled and chopped butternut squash into a bowl and mix together with the 2 tbsp olive oil, salt, black pepper and paprika.
3 Place on a lined baking tray and bake in the oven for 25-30 minutes or until slightly browned.
4 Wash the lentils then place in a saucepan with the water. Bring to the boil and then simmer uncovered for 20-30 minutes. Drain and then use for assembly.

French Dressing
1 Place all ingredients in a blender and blend until smooth.
2 If using a jam jar, crush the garlic and place in the jar with the other ingredients. Shake until thoroughly combined.

Assembly (for 1 serving)
1 Create a bed of rocket or salad leaves on a large dinner plate.
2 Scatter one quarter of the cooked lentils over the leaves.
3 Arrange pieces of the roasted squash over the lentils.
4 Cover with a small amount of French dressing.

Optional: crumble with a handful of vegan Greek-style cheese, toasted seeds and marinated tofu.

All kitted out
- Saucepan • Vegetable peeler • Large knife
- Chopping board • Baking tray • Baking paper
- Blender or jam jar (with lid)

Helpful hint: for a speedy version, buy pre-cut pieces of butternut squash and/or pre-cooked lentils (eg Merchant Gourmet) and ready-made French dressing.

Sides
Crispy, Spicy Chickpeas

Serves 4 | 45 minutes or less

- 2 tins chickpeas (drained, rinsed and thoroughly dried off. Keep the liquid – aquafaba – as it's useful as an egg replacer in baking – it freezes well too)
- 6 tbsp ground cumin
- 4 tbsp garlic powder
- 4 tsp ground coriander
- 1 tsp ground ginger
- 4 tsp paprika
- Salt (to taste)
- 2-3 tbsp olive oil

1 Pre-heat the oven to 200°C/400°F/Gas Mark 6.
2 Add chickpeas to the mixing bowl and toss with oil, salt and spices.
3 Place on a lined baking tray and bake for 20-25 minutes or until golden and crispy.
4 Serve with salads, soup or enjoy as a snack on their own.

All kitted out
- Mixing bowl • Measuring spoons • Sieve • Kitchen roll • Baking tray • Baking paper

Speedy Marinated Tofu

Serves 2-4 | 45 minutes or less

- 100ml/¼ cup + 2tbsp olive oil
- 28g/1oz parsley (with stalks)
- 2 cloves garlic (peeled and roughly chopped)
- 25ml tamari or other soy sauce
- 300g/11oz (approx) firm tofu
- 2 tbsp nutritional yeast flakes

1 Pre-heat the oven to 180°C/350°F/Gas Mark 4-5.
2 Drain the water from the tofu and wrap the block in a clean tea towel or several sheets of kitchen roll. Leave for 20 minutes to absorb as much water as possible.
3 Blend together the olive oil, parsley and garlic using a blender or stick blender.
4 Line a large baking tray with baking parchment.
5 Slice the tofu width ways about 0.5cm/¼ inch thick.
6 Lay the tofu on the lined baking tray.
7 Pour the garlic and parsley sauce, then the tamari, evenly over each slice.
8 Place the tray into the oven for 15-20 minutes.
9 Take the tray out then turn each slice of tofu, adding a bit more tamari if necessary.
10 Sprinkle the nutritional yeast evenly over all slices and bake for a further 5-10 minutes.

All kitted out
- Kitchen paper or clean tea towel • Blender • Baking tray • Baking paper • Knife • Chopping board

Mains

Aubergine Towers with Roasted Tomato, Red Pepper & Onion Sauce

Serves 4 | 1 hour or less

This is an old Viva! favourite. We've simplified the recipe and broken it down into easy steps. Basically, while the main components are baking in the oven you do a bit of stovetop and blender action! The dish is lovely served with roast potatoes – white or sweet – or a grain such as rice or quinoa.

Aubergine slices to roast
- 2 medium-large aubergines
- 2 tbsp olive oil

Roasted Tomato, Red Pepper & Onion Sauce
- 2 tbsp olive oil
- 450g/1lb large ripe tomatoes, roughly chopped
- 1 red pepper, deseeded and roughly chopped
- 1 onion, roughly chopped
- 2 garlic cloves, roughly chopped
- 1 tsp dried mixed herbs or the equivalent – eg thyme, oregano, sage mixed together
- Salt and black pepper

Filling
- 1 small onion, chopped, any colour

- 2 garlic cloves, crushed or 1 tsp garlic purée
- 2 medium-large aubergines, peeled and chopped
- 2 tsp lemon zest
- 1 tsp ground cumin
- ½ tsp ground cinnamon
- 50g/¼ cup sultanas or raisins
- 50g/¼ cup roasted cashew nuts
- 2 tsp tahini
- 50g (about 8) sundried tomatoes, drained and chopped with scissors
- Fresh coriander or parsley – a tablespoon or two
- Salt and pepper

1 Pre-heat the oven to 200°C/400°F/Gas Mark 6.
2 Slice the two medium-large aubergines into large circular chunks to make 16 slices for the towers. They need to be approx 2-3cm/generous 1 inch deep.
3 Place 2 tbsp oil on one of the roasting trays and toss the aubergine slices on this then sprinkle with salt and set aside.
4 Now prep the sauce. Chop the sauce vegetables roughly, place on the second baking tray and toss them in the oil so that everything is well coated. Place in the oven along with the tray of aubergine slices.
5 Set the timer for 20-25 minutes. Check after 15 and turn the aubergine slices.
6 Meanwhile, make the filling. Peel and chop the aubergine and set aside.
7 In a saucepan, sauté the onion and garlic until soft, stirring so the garlic doesn't catch. Add the spices.

Reduce the heat a little and add a splash of hot water to the pan if it starts to catch. Add the chopped aubergine plus the sultanas or raisins, tahini, lemon zest, sundried tomatoes and coriander.
8 When the filling mixture is cooked and tender, add the cashews. Taste and add more salt if necessary. Keep warm.
9 Check the two roasting trays in the oven. The aubergine slices should be tender and golden but not too soft. The roast vegetables should be softened and squidgy. Return either or both trays to the oven for another 5-10 minutes or so if necessary.
10 Make the sauce. Remove the sauce veg from the oven and blend until smooth. Taste and adjust seasoning if necessary. Reduce oven temperature by about half until the dish is ready to serve.
11 Place the largest pieces of aubergine on the bottom of each plate and then layer with some of the filling. Repeat this until you have 'towers' – see our photograph! (Keep any leftover filling and add to the plates when serving.)
12 Serve with the sauce, the extra stuffing and any accompaniments. Eat while hot.

All kitted out
- 2 roasting trays or equivalent • Chopping board and knife • Measuring spoons • Kettle • Medium saucepan and lid • Cooking spoon • Blender or food processor • Small saucepan • Spatula • 'Fish' slice/turner

Chik'n & Mushroom Pasties – with mushroomphobes' alternative

Makes 4 pasties | 45 minutes

Comfort food at its best. (If you think mushrooms are the work of the devil, we offer a replacement! See the ingredients list.)

- 1 tbsp olive oil
- ½ a leek cut lengthways then sliced into semi-circles. Wash thoroughly in a colander in running water to dislodge grit
- 1 large garlic clove, crushed
- ¼ pack vegan chicken pieces, eg Quorn vegan chicken or Fry's chicken-style strips
- 150g/2 cups sliced mushrooms (OR 150g small cubes of squash or sweet potato with an added 1-2 tsp medium miso)
- 2 tbsp finely chopped fresh tarragon or parsley or 1 tsp dried
- 150ml/½ cup unsweetened plant milk, eg soya or almond, plus a little extra for glazing
- 1½ tsp arrowroot, mixed into a paste with a few tablespoons of the plant milk
- 50ml/¼ cup vegan stock
- 2 tbsp vegan cream
- Salt and lots of black pepper
- Pasties: 1 sheet of ready-rolled vegan puff pastry cut into 4, eg JusRol, Sainsbury's, Tesco, Aldi etc – look for the green packets, which are usually butter-free
- Pies: 1 sheet of ready-rolled vegan shortcrust pastry (blue pack) to line ramekins and 1 sheet ready-rolled puff pastry for pie lids
- A little oil or oil spray for the pasty trays

To serve: mash, gravy and any side vegetables of your choice.

1 Preheat the oven to 200°C/400°F/Gas Mark 6.
2 Heat the oil in the saucepan/wok and gently fry the leek pieces for a few minutes then add the garlic. Add the mushrooms or alternative and cook for another few minutes. If using squash/sweet potato option, ensure that it is completely cooked before proceeding.
3 Add the vegan chicken and fry that in for a minute or two, plus the herbs.
4 If using the miso, mix it into a paste with 2-3 tablespoons of the stock and add now.
5 Add the arrowroot paste, cooking it in and stirring to prevent lumps – drizzle the plant milk in slowly to stop the mixture from going lumpy. Add the stock also and stir in well. Cook for 2-3 minutes to cook in the arrowroot.
6 Add the cream, taste and season well. Taste again, adjusting the seasoning if necessary.
7 Place the four pieces of pastry on to the baking sheet. Spoon the filling equally on to each piece. Brush round the edges of each piece with the plant milk then fold over each one to create a pasty. Seal each pasty by pressing down with your thumbs all around the edges.

8 Pierce each pasty once with a sharp knife and lightly brush the tops with the rest of the plant milk.
9 Place in the oven immediately and bake for 15-20 minutes until golden and the pastry is properly cooked.

All kitted out
• 1-2 oven trays for pasties (if trays have lost their non-stick qualities, line with crumpled baking paper)
• A saucepan or wok plus cooking spoon • Chopping board and knife • Colander • Small bowl • Measuring scales or cups • Measuring spoon • Measuring jug • Vegetable peeler • Pastry brush

All kitted out

• Large saucepan and cooking spoon • Chopping board and knife • Measuring cups or scales • Measuring spoons • Tin opener • Citrus squeezer

Smoky Chilli Hotpot with Black Beans, Lentils & Chocolate

Serves 4-6 | 30-40 minutes

This is a simple, hearty dish that lends itself to bulk cooking. We've used tinned beans and lentils for speed but feel free to use home-cooked pulses.

Cacao and chocolate have been used as savoury flavourings in Central America for a very long time. They add a dark and rich flavour rather than sweet and milky! Use cacao or cocoa – or even a few squares of very dark bitter chocolate. (Cacao is unrefined cocoa and is now available mainstream).

- 1 onion, any colour, chopped into smallish pieces or slices
- 3 large cloves garlic, crushed or chopped
- ¼-½ tsp chilli powder, depending on personal taste and how hot the powder is
- 2 tsp cumin seeds
- 1 tsp cinnamon
- 1 tsp coriander powder
- 1 tsp smoked paprika
- 1½ celery sticks, chopped
- 1½ medium carrots, chopped
- 1 large red pepper, deseeded and chopped
- 1 tin brown or green lentils, drained (400ml/14oz tin)
- 1 tin black beans (400ml/14oz tin)
- 500ml/generous 2 cups passata
- 180-300ml/¾-1¼ cups strong vegan stock – start with a little and add more if needed
- 2 tsp cacao or cocoa powder OR 2-3 squares of 70-80% dark vegan chocolate
- Juice of ½-1 lime
- 1½ tsp date syrup, agave or dark brown sugar
- Salt and pepper to taste

Serving suggestions
- Chopped coriander or parsley
- Guacamole – mashed avocado with garlic, salt and lime
- Vegan sour cream or vegan crème fraiche, eg Oatly
- Tortillas
- Hot pepper sauce for the heat-lovers!

1 Heat the oil in the saucepan and gently fry the onion for a few minutes until softened. Add the spices and garlic and fry in for 2 minutes, stirring well. Add the celery, carrots and red pepper and cook slowly for 7-10 minutes. Make sure everything is mixed in well. Add a splash or two of stock if it starts to stick.

2 Add the passata and the minimum amount of stock and stir in. Cook for about 10-15 minutes on a simmer or until the vegetables have softened.

3 Add the cooked lentils and beans. Stir again, adding more stock if needed.

4 Add the cacao, cocoa or chocolate, the syrup or brown sugar and the lime juice. Cook for another five minutes. Taste and add more stock powder, salt or lime juice if necessary. Serve hot with all the trimmings.

Creamy Leek, Celeriac & Walnut Pies

Serves 4 | 1 hour
Creates 4 individual pies using 150-200ml ramekins or foil pie cases

- ½-1 celeriac (peeled and cubed into ½ inch pieces)
- 3-4 tbsp water
- 4 tbsp olive oil
- Salt
- Freshly ground pepper
- 1 leek, finely sliced
- 3 cloves garlic, crushed
- 1 tsp paprika
- 50g walnut pieces (lightly toasted in the oven for 10 minutes at 180°C)
- 1 sheet of ready-rolled shortcrust pastry (eg JusRol) AND 1 sheet of ready-rolled puff pastry (eg JusRol)
- Small amount of soya milk for glazing the pastry

Sauce
- 130g/1 cup raw cashews (unsalted and unroasted and preferably whole, not pieces) soaked in a bowl of cold water and covered – for at least 2 hours but up to 8. Doing it overnight is the easiest way!
- 120-180ml/½-¾ cup water
- Fine salt to taste – just a pinch. Add gradually, mix in thoroughly after each addition and remember that sea salt is stronger than regular
- 2 tbsp vegan white wine
- 3 fresh sage leaves
- Juice of half a lemon
- 1 tsp stock powder (or add more to taste if you like a stronger flavour… do it bit by bit though or it will be too salty!)
- 1 tbsp nutritional yeast

Filling
1 Heat one tablespoon of olive oil in a large saucepan and then add the leek pieces. Cook with a lid on for around 8-10 minutes but check they are not sticking or burning.
2 Add the cubed celeriac, garlic, a pinch of salt, paprika and 3 tablespoons of olive oil.
3 Lightly fry for a few minutes then add the water. Place a lid on top then cook for around 20 minutes or until the celeriac is tender.
4 Add the toasted walnuts, taste and season accordingly with salt and freshly ground pepper.

Sauce
1 Soak the cashews (for a minimum of 2 hours or overnight).
2 Put all ingredients into a blender and blend until really smooth, adding water a little at a time. The more you add the thinner the cream will be - although the cream will thicken when left to stand in its container. Keep blending and scraping down the sides until the mixture is very smooth and creamy and has lost its grainy texture.
3 Transfer the mixture to a medium-sized pan and bring to the boil and then simmer until heated through (approx 5-10 minutes). Add more stock/fluid if necessary/to taste.

Assembly

1 Pre-heat the oven to 200°C/400°F/Gas Mark 6.
2 Oil each ramekin then line with a layer of shortcrust ready to roll pastry.
3 Blind bake them in the oven for 10 minutes, covering them with greaseproof paper weighed down with baking beans or rice.
4 Leave them to cool for 10 minutes then add the celeriac and leek filling until the pie is full.
5 Spoon approximately 5 tablespoons of cashew sauce into each pie (or to your taste).
6 Take the puff pastry and cut a circular lid for each of the pies. If you don't have pastry cutters, you can use a bowl or top of a glass (if it fits).
7 Cover each of the pies with the puff pastry lid and seal them by sticking the puff pastry lid to the shortcrust base.
8 Brush the lids with a thin layer of soya milk and then bake in the oven until risen and golden (approx 20-30 minutes).

All kitted out

- 4 x 150-200ml ramekins or 4 foil pie cases (180ml)
- Large saucepan with lid • Chopping board
- Sharp knife • Measuring spoons • Blender
- Small spatula • Medium saucepan • Pastry cutters or medium-sized bowl • Bowl for soaking cashews and weighing equipment

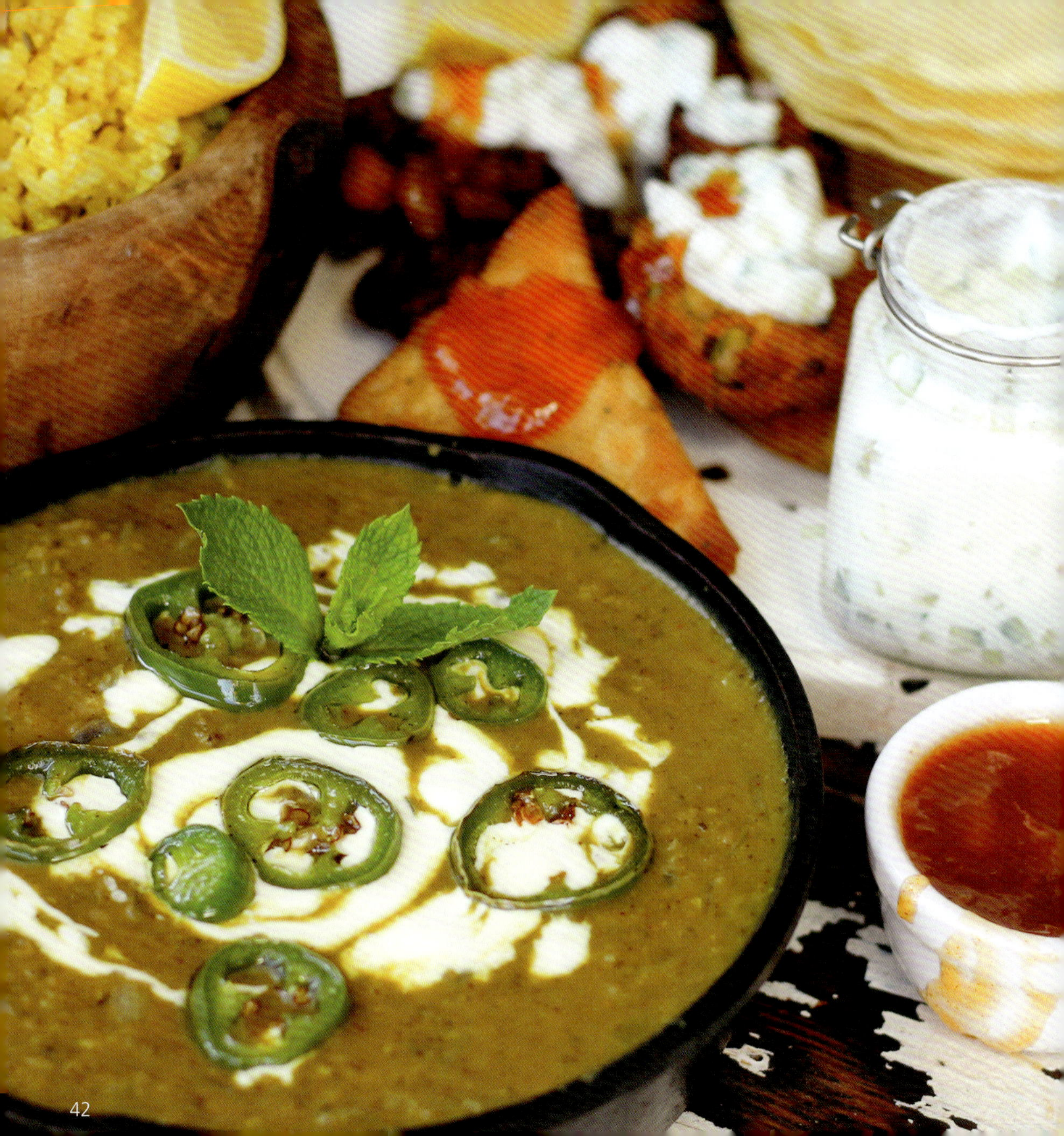

Deep & Mellow Masoor Dhal

Serves 4-6 | 30-40 minutes

With its deep flavours of cardamom, clove, cinnamon and cumin and the addition of coconut cream, this is a fragrant, comforting and satisfying dish. We like it with other curry dishes and rice – or just served with rice and lightly sautéed, garlic-flavoured winter greens (eg dark green cabbage, shredded Brussels sprouts or broccoli). The dhal also freezes very well.

NB coconut cream is like very thick coconut milk – not to be confused with creamed coconut which is sold in hard blocks!

- 225g/1 cup red lentils (masoor dhal)
- 1 tsp salt
- 2 tbsp plain vegetable oil
- 2 onions, chopped
- 125ml (half a pack) of Blue Dragon coconut cream or 1 small tin, eg Waitrose

Masala paste

- 1 tsp cumin seeds
- 1 tsp poppy seeds
- ½ tsp chilli powder or 1 tsp paprika
- 1 tsp turmeric powder
- 2 tsp coriander seeds
- 6 cloves
- 5cm/2 inch cinnamon stick
- 4 green cardamoms, split and seeds removed
- 4 black peppercorns
- 4 cloves garlic

1 Wash the lentils and leave them to soak while you prepare the rest of the ingredients.
2 Grind up all the ingredients for the masala paste.
3 Chop the onions.
4 Drain the lentils and put them into the pan along with the salt and enough water to cover, plus about 2cm/1 inch over. Bring to the boil and simmer. Skim off excess froth.
5 Cook for 15-20 minutes until the lentils are soft. Stir and check water levels occasionally.
6 Meanwhile, cook in the masala paste. Heat the oil in the smaller pan. Sauté the onions on a low heat until golden and soft for 5-10 minutes. Add a aplash of water if they start to stick. Add the masala paste and fry with the onion mix for 2 minutes. Remove from heat.
7 When the lentils are soft and creamy, add the masala paste mixture and the coconut cream. Mix in well. Taste and adjust seasoning if necessary. Serve hot.

All kitted out

- Sieve • Medium-large saucepan and cooking spoon
- Medium-small saucepan and spoon • Chopping board and knife • Frying pan and 'fish' slice/turner
- Measuring scales or cups • Measuring jug or cups
- Measuring spoons • Spice grinder or small blender
- Small bowl

Hazelnut Pasta Pesto

Serves 4 | 30 minutes

- 400g wholewheat spaghetti
- Salt

Hazelnut Pesto
- 150g hazelnuts (with or without skins)
- 80g fresh basil
- 2 cloves garlic (peeled)
- 2 tbsp lemon juice
- 200ml olive oil
- 1 tbsp vegan syrup (eg maple, agave)
- Salt & pepper to taste

Plus
- Fresh basil
- Cherry tomatoes
- Vegan parmesan or Greek-style cheese

1 Pre-heat the oven to 200°C/400°F/Gas Mark 6. Heat a panful of water for the pasta.
2 Place the hazelnuts on a baking tray and roast in the oven for 5-10 minutes. Be careful they don't burn.
3 If the hazelnuts are skinned go to stage 4. If not, put them in a clean tea towel and rub them together to remove the skins.
4 Place the hazelnuts in a blender and then pulse until roughly chopped but not smooth.
5 Add all the other pesto ingredients into the blender and pulse, but leave fairly chunky.
6 Add the spaghetti to the boiling water, then simmer according to instructions on the packet.
7 Drain the spaghetti and stir the pesto into the warm pasta.
8 Serve with fresh basil, cherry tomatoes and vegan parmesan or Greek-style cheese.

All kitted out
- Baking tray • Clean tea towel • Scales • Measuring spoons • Measuring jug • Blender • Saucepan

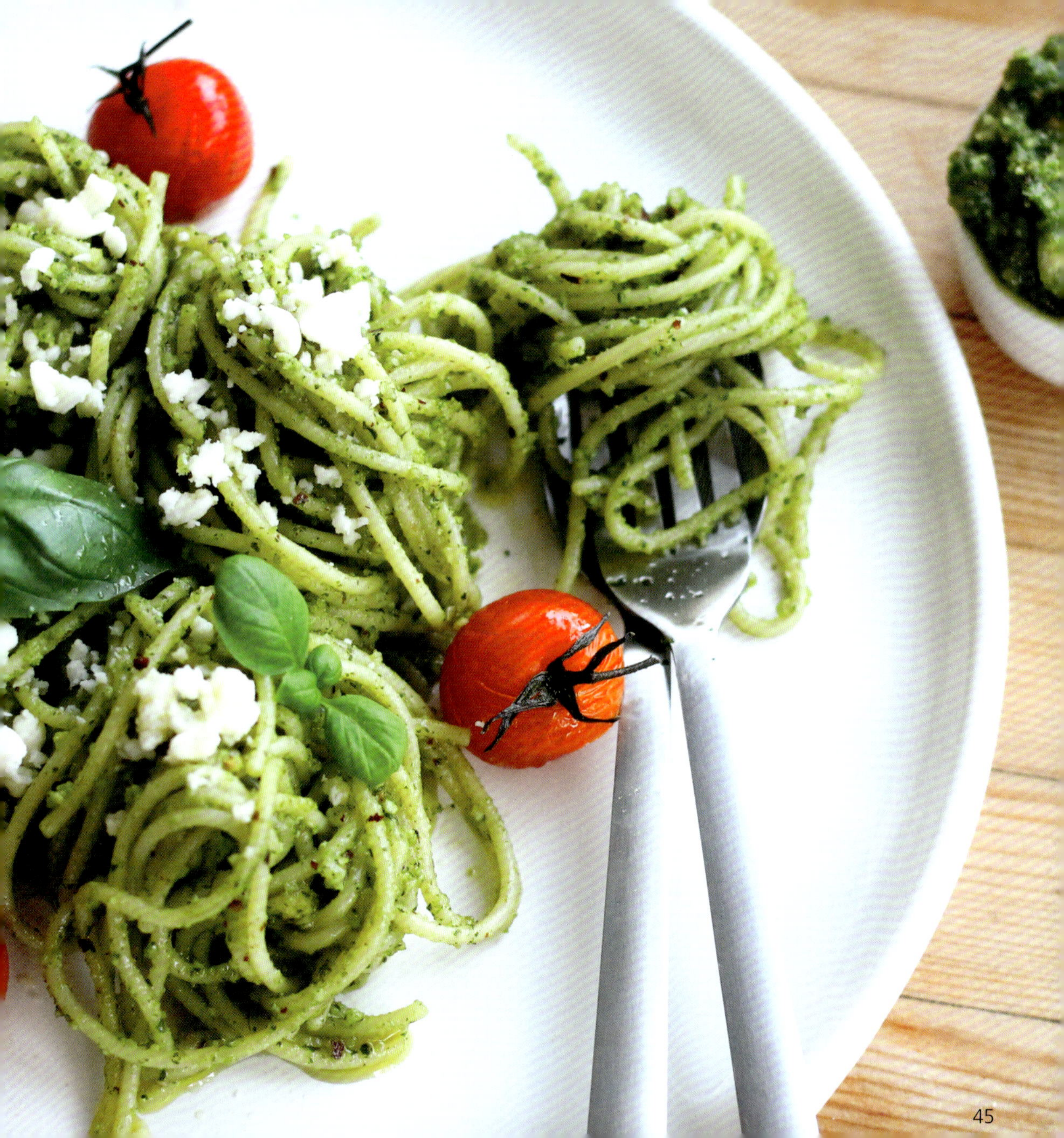

Moussaka

Serves 4 | 1-2 hours

Aubergines
- 6 aubergines
- Olive oil
- Salt

Filling
- Olive oil
- 2 onions, finely diced
- 3 cloves garlic, finely diced
- 250g mushrooms, sliced
- 500g vegan soya mince (frozen)
- 1-2 tbsp tomato purée
- 2 (400g) tins chopped tomatoes
- 150ml vegan red wine
- 150ml stock
- 1 tsp dried oregano
- ½ tsp cinnamon
- 1 tbsp vegan syrup (eg maple, agave)

Béchamel
- 4 tbsp vegan margarine
- 4 tbsp plain flour
- 400ml unsweetened soya milk
- 2 tsp Dijon mustard
- Pinch of grated nutmeg
- 1-2 tsp salt (to taste)
- 2 tsp egg replacer, eg Orgran (optional)
- 150g silken tofu (optional)
- 1 tbsp nutritional yeast (optional)

Topping
- Melting vegan cheese eg Violife Mozzarella or Greek-style Cheese
- Vegan parmesan eg Violife Prosociano, Parma or supermarket own brand

Aubergines
1 Pre-heat the oven to 200°C/400°F/Gas Mark 6.
2 Remove stalks and cut the aubergines into slices, 1cm thick.
3 Season with salt and drizzle with olive oil.
4 Place on baking tray and cook, turning once, for 20-30 minutes or until soft and golden.

Filling
1 Fry the onion in a little oil until lightly golden.
2 Add the mushrooms and cook until slightly softened.
3 Add the garlic, oregano, cinnamon and fry for a further 1-2 minutes.
4 Stir in the tomato purée, veggie mince, red wine, stock, tinned tomatoes and syrup. Bring to the boil, turn down the heat and simmer with the lid on for roughly 30 minutes, until most of the liquid has evaporated.
5 Salt and sweeten to taste.

Béchamel
1 Using a large saucepan, melt the margarine on a low heat.
2 Take the saucepan off the heat and stir in the flour until you have a paste.
3 Return the pan to the heat, turn up to medium and very gradually add the soya milk, stirring continuously to avoid lumps.
4 Once the sauce has thickened, add the Dijon, nutmeg, salt and optional extras (if using). Use a balloon whisk to get rid of lumps if necessary.
5 Stir thoroughly then set aside.

Assembly
1 Reduce the oven heat to 180°C/350°F/Gas Mark 4-5.
2 Place a layer of aubergine into a greased, rectangular oven dish followed by a layer of the filling.
3 Repeat this process until you have several layers.
4 Leaving a couple of inches at the top, pour on the béchamel sauce so that the top of the moussaka is completely covered.
5 Add a thick layer of melting vegan cheese.
6 Cover with foil and bake in the oven for 25 minutes.
7 Remove from the oven, take off the foil, sprinkle over the parmesan and place back in the oven, uncovered, for a further 15 minutes until the top is slightly browned.

All kitted out
- Scales • Chopping board • Sharp knife • Measuring jug • Measuring spoons • Large, deep frying pan • Large saucepan • Wooden spoons • Rectangular oven-proof dish • Baking tray

Rockin' Moroccan Sweet Potato Tagine with Preserved Lemons & Olives

Serves 4 | 40 minutes

Simple and good. The secret with this is not to overcook the sweet potato – you want it just cooked and no more.

- 2 tbsp olive oil
- 2 large red onions, sliced
- 3 garlic cloves, crushed or chopped
- 1 tbsp peeled and grated fresh ginger – use the edge of a teaspoon for quick peeling
- 2 large or 3 medium sweet potatoes, peeled and cut into large chunks
- 1 tin chickpeas, drained and rinsed (freeze or fridge the bean water for baking, mayo, meringues etc)
- 1½ tsp ground cinnamon
- ½ tsp turmeric powder
- 1 tsp cumin powder
- 1 tsp agave syrup
- ½ red chilli, deseeded and chopped small
- 2 small preserved lemons, finely chopped
- 2 tsp vegan bouillon or 1 stock cube, low salt
- About 10 pitted olives, any colour, chopped
- 100g/½ cup dried apricots, finely chopped
- Fresh lemon juice to taste, 1-2 tbsp. Add more if desired
- Fresh coriander or parsley, finely chopped – a few tablespoons

To serve: cooked quinoa, couscous or bulgur wheat – or just some nice flatbread to mop up the juices!

1 Heat the oil in the saucepan and sauté the onion for a few minutes until softened. Add the garlic, ginger, sweet potato chunks and chickpeas. Cook for about 5 minutes.

2 Add the cinnamon, turmeric, cumin, chilli, agave, preserved lemons and stock powder or crumbled cube. Cook this in for a minute or two.

3 Add the sweet potato and cover with boiling water – approximately 500ml/2 cups. Bring to the boil and simmer for a few minutes, covered. Keep an eye on the sweet potatoes – check after 3-4 minutes and test them.

4 Add the olives and apricots and heat through for a minute or two. Add a splash of hot water if the mixture is beginning to dry out too much. The tagine is ready when the sweet potatoes are just tender.

5 Add most of the fresh herbs and the lemon juice. Taste, adjust the seasoning if necessary and stir. Serve hot, with the remaining herbs and grains/breads of choice.

All kitted out
- Chopping board and knife • Vegetable peeler
- Measuring scales or cups • Measuring spoons
- Citrus squeezer • Tin opener • Kettle of boiling water
- Medium-large saucepan and cooking spoon
- Large serving spoon

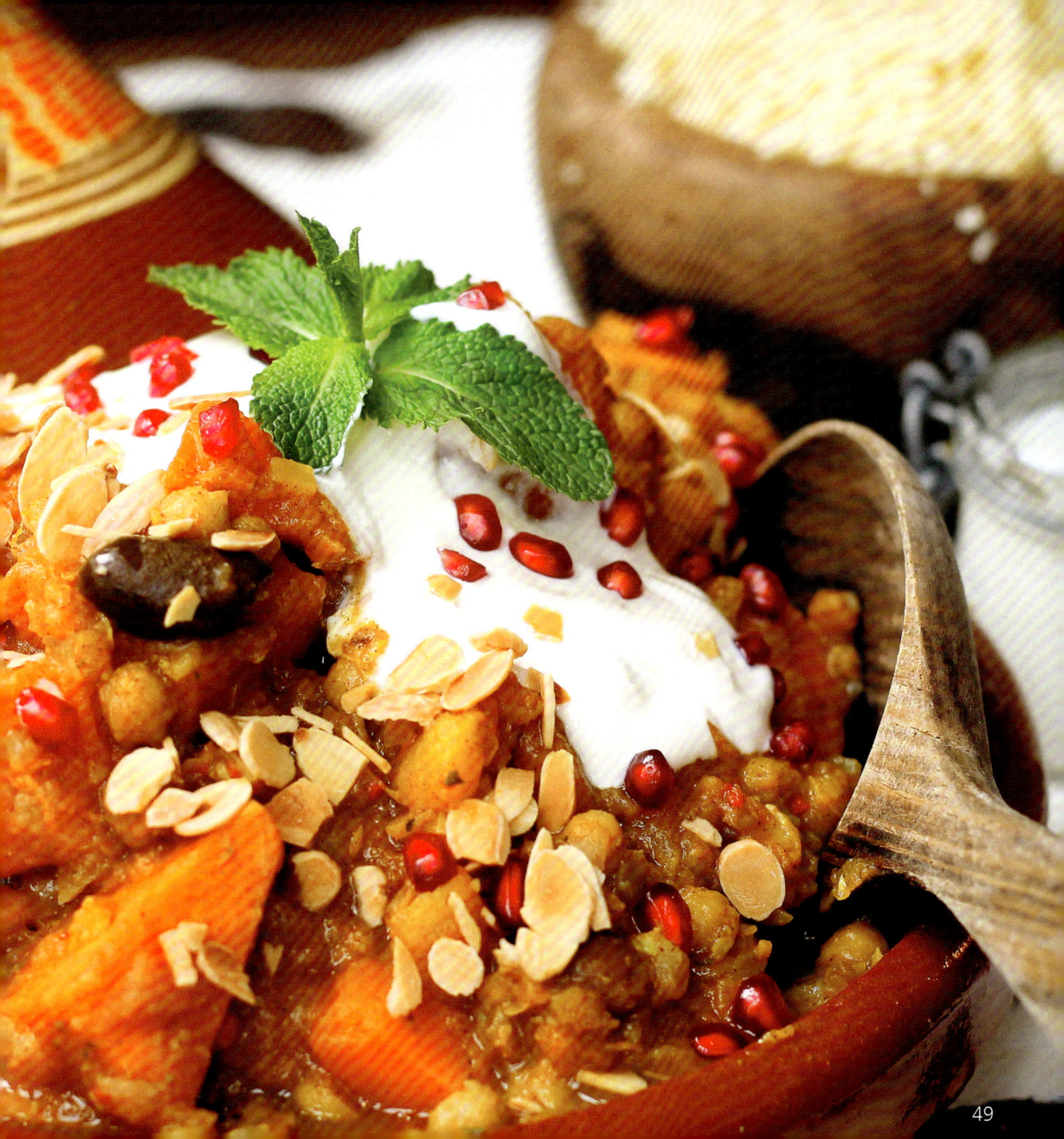

All kitted out
- Chopping board • Sharp knife • Large saucepan
- Wooden spoon • Measuring spoons • Measuring jug
- Medium saucepan • Kitchen paper or clean tea towel • Sieve • 2 x wide bowls

Tofu Katsu Curry

Serves 4 | 45 minutes

- 400g brown/wholegrain rice

Sauce
- 1 tbsp vegetable oil
- 2 onions, finely diced
- 5 cloves garlic, finely diced
- 4 carrots, peeled and chopped
- 4 tbsp plain flour
- 2 tbsp medium curry powder
- 1 tsp garam masala
- 1200ml/5L stock
- 1 tbsp vegan syrup (eg maple, agave)
- 2 bay leaves
- 2 tbsp soya sauce

Tofu
- 800g/28-30oz firm tofu (eg 2 packets of Cauldron or similar)
- 240g/8-9oz panko breadcrumbs (eg 2 packets of Blue Dragon)
- 5 tbsp plain flour
- 5 tbsp water
- Vegetable oil for deep frying

Sauce

1 Heat the oil in a large saucepan and add the onion. Sauté for a couple of minutes.
2 Add the carrots and sweat for 10-15 minutes (with the lid on) until they soften and begin to caramelise.
3 Add the garlic and stir for a further minute.
4 Stir in the flour, garam masala and curry powder and cook for a minute.
5 Pour in the stock slowly and gradually to avoid lumps.
6 Add the soya sauce, vegan syrup and bay leaf. Bring to the boil then reduce the heat and simmer for 20-30 minutes so the sauce has thickened but is still pouring consistency.
7 You can either keep the sauce chunky or pass through a sieve if you prefer it smooth.

Tofu

1 Unwrap the tofu, drain and place in a colander. Cover with a clean tea towel or kitchen towel, then a plate. Place weights or tins of food on top. Let it drain over the sink and leave for 30 minutes minimum.
2 Slice each block of tofu in half lengthways.
3 Mix the flour and water into a paste in a wide bowl and set aside.
4 Empty the panko breadcrumbs into a wide bowl and set aside.
5 Dip each chunk of tofu into the flour/water paste and make sure it is thoroughly covered.
6 Then dip the tofu into the bowl of panko breadcrumbs until thoroughly covered.
7 Heat a medium saucepan half full of vegetable oil on medium-high heat or use a deep fat fryer.
8 Lower the tofu chunks into the hot fat and cook for a few minutes or until golden brown and crispy.
9 Remove each piece with a slotted turner and place on kitchen roll to soak up the excess oil until ready to serve.

Assembly

1 Serve on a bed of rice.
2 Slice the tofu and drizzle with the curry sauce.
3 Optional: garnish with chillis, carrot and spring onion.

Ultimate Vegan Pizza

Serves 8 | 1½ hours (including time for dough to prove)

Dough
- 500g strong white bread flour
- ½ tbsp salt
- 7g sachet/1½ tsp of fast action dried yeast
- 1 tbsp golden caster sugar
- 2 tbsp extra virgin olive oil
- 325ml lukewarm water

Tomato Sauce
(If you're short of time, use a shop-bought passata or dairy-free pesto eg La Sacla, Meridian, Zest)
- Olive oil
- 2 cloves garlic, finely diced
- 400g (2 tins) plum tomatoes
- Pinch of salt

Topping
- Melting vegan cheese… our favourite melting varieties are: Violife Mozzarella, Bute Island Sheeze Mozzarella, Bute Island Greek Style Sheese, Tesco and Sainsbury's Greek Style, or MozzaRisella
- Choose from your favourite toppings and get creative

The pizza pictured above has a topping of:
- Greek Style Sheese (see melting cheese details)
- Homemade tomato sauce (recipe above)
- Caramelised red onion
- Black olives (pitted)

Dough
1 Sieve the flour and salt into a large bowl and make a well (hole) in the middle.
2 In a jug, mix the yeast, sugar, oil and water and leave for a few minutes, then pour into the well.
3 Bring the flour in gradually from the sides and stir it into the liquid using a fork. Keep mixing, drawing larger amounts of flour in, and when it all starts to come together, work the rest of the flour in with your clean, flour-dusted hands. Knead until you have a smooth, springy dough.
4 Place the ball of dough in a large flour-dusted bowl and flour the top of it. Cover the bowl with a damp cloth and prove (place in a warm room for about an hour until the dough has doubled in size).
5 Now remove the dough to a flour-dusted surface and knead it a bit to push the air out with your hands. You can either use it immediately, or keep it, wrapped in clingfilm, in the fridge (or freezer) until required.
6 If using straight away, divide the dough up into as many little balls as you want to make pizzas – this amount of dough is enough to make about 3-4 medium pizzas.
7 Use the dough straight away unless storing.
8 Roll out into whatever shape you fancy (circle- ish) until the dough is about ½ cm/just under ½ inch thick. It should be springy but not sticky.

Tomato Sauce (this can be made in advance or while the pizza dough is proving)
1 Heat a tablespoon of olive oil in a pan on a low-medium heat and then add the chopped garlic.

2 Cook for a minute or two until the garlic is light golden in colour.
3 Add the tomatoes, a pinch of salt and leave on a low-med heat for 20-25 minutes.
4 Give it a final stir, breaking up the tomatoes with a spoon.

Assembly
1 Heat oven to 250°C/480°F/Gas Mark 9.
2 Spread the sauce, passata or pesto onto the freshly rolled (uncooked) dough.
3 Add the cheese first (this prevents the toppings sliding off).
4 Add a combination of toppings.
5 Put in the oven for 7-10 minutes until golden and crisp.

All kitted out
• Large mixing bowl • Measuring jug • Measuring spoons • Chopping board • Sharp knife • Medium saucepan • Wooden spoon • Baking tray • Baking paper

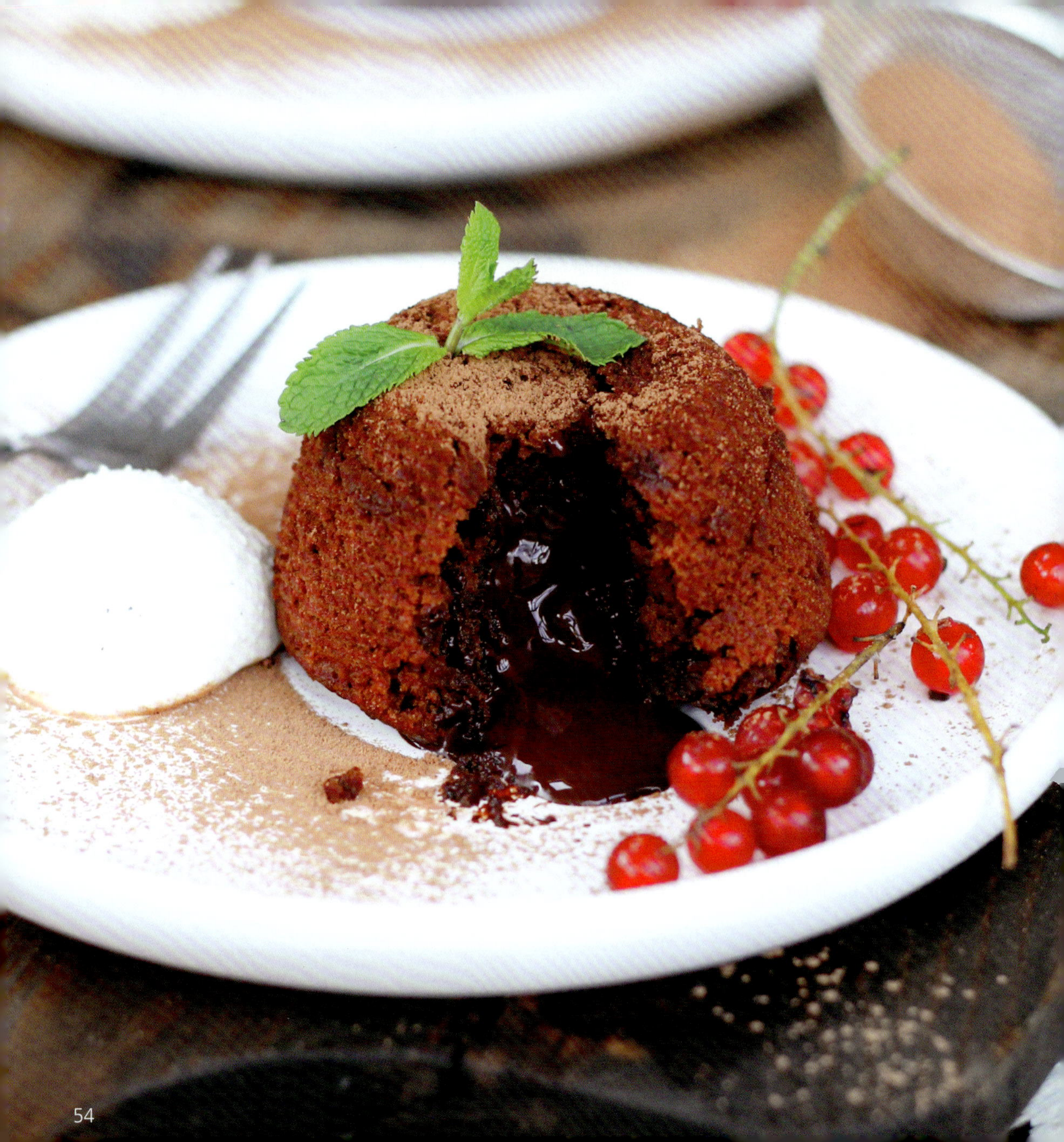

Desserts

Chocolate Fondants

Serves 4 | 30 minutes

Wet Ingredients
- 145ml almond milk
- 75g vegan margarine
- ¾ tsp cider vinegar
- 2½ tbsp apple sauce
- Splash of vanilla essence

Dry Ingredients
- 145g plain flour
- 120g caster sugar
- 3 tbsp raw cacao or cocoa powder
- 2 tsp (flat) baking powder
- Pinch salt

Filling
- 100-150g vegan dark chocolate of your choice

To serve
- Cacao or cocoa powder
- Vegan ice cream
- Redcurrants or other berries for decoration

1 Pre-heat the oven to 180°/350°F/Gas Mark 4.
2 Grease 4 pudding basins.
3 Place all the wet ingredients into a saucepan and gently heat on a low-medium heat, stirring until melted and blended.
4 In a large mixing bowl, sieve the flour and add all the dry ingredients, stirring until thoroughly combined.
5 Fold the wet ingredients into the dry ingredients until combined.
6 Fill the pudding basins with the mixture until ¾ full.
7 Push 5 pieces of chocolate into the middle of each of the basins until they are fully submerged.
8 Place them on a baking tray and bake in the oven for 12-15 minutes.
9 Sprinkle with cacao/cocoa powder and serve hot with ice cream and red currants.

All kitted out
- Scales • Measuring spoons • Saucepan • Measuring jug • Large mixing bowl • Sieve • Mixing spoons
- 4 pudding basins (209ml) • Baking tray

Cinder Toffee

Serves 4-6 | 2¼ hours (including setting time, otherwise very quick!)

- 200g/⅞ cup caster sugar
- 8 tbsp golden syrup
- 3 tsp bicarbonate of soda
- 200g/1¼ cup vegan chocolate (optional)

1 Place the syrup and sugar into a saucepan and stir to thoroughly mix. Don't continue stirring once the pan is on the heat.
2 Heat up the mixture on a medium heat and let the mixture melt first. Then let it turn to a gooey consistency, then to bubbling. Stir gently and wait for it to turn a golden colour, similar to maple syrup. This will take around 3 minutes. Don't overheat the mixture or it can develop a bitter taste.
3 Take the pan off the heat, whisk in the bicarbonate of soda and wait for the mixture to puff up. Let it increase in size and become aerated. Empty the mixture immediately onto a lined baking tray.
4 Leave until set (around 2 hours) and then break it up into bite-size chunks.

Optional: melt the vegan chocolate using a double boiler (see ALL KITTED OUT) then dip individual chunks of the cinder toffee into it. Make sure the chocolate is not too hot to touch. Leave it to cool/set.

All kitted out
- Mixing bowl • Measuring spoons • Large saucepan
- Wooden spoon • Baking tray • Baking paper
- Double boiler (only if melting chocolate) – a glass or ceramic bowl that fits on a saucepan of water but doesn't touch the bottom

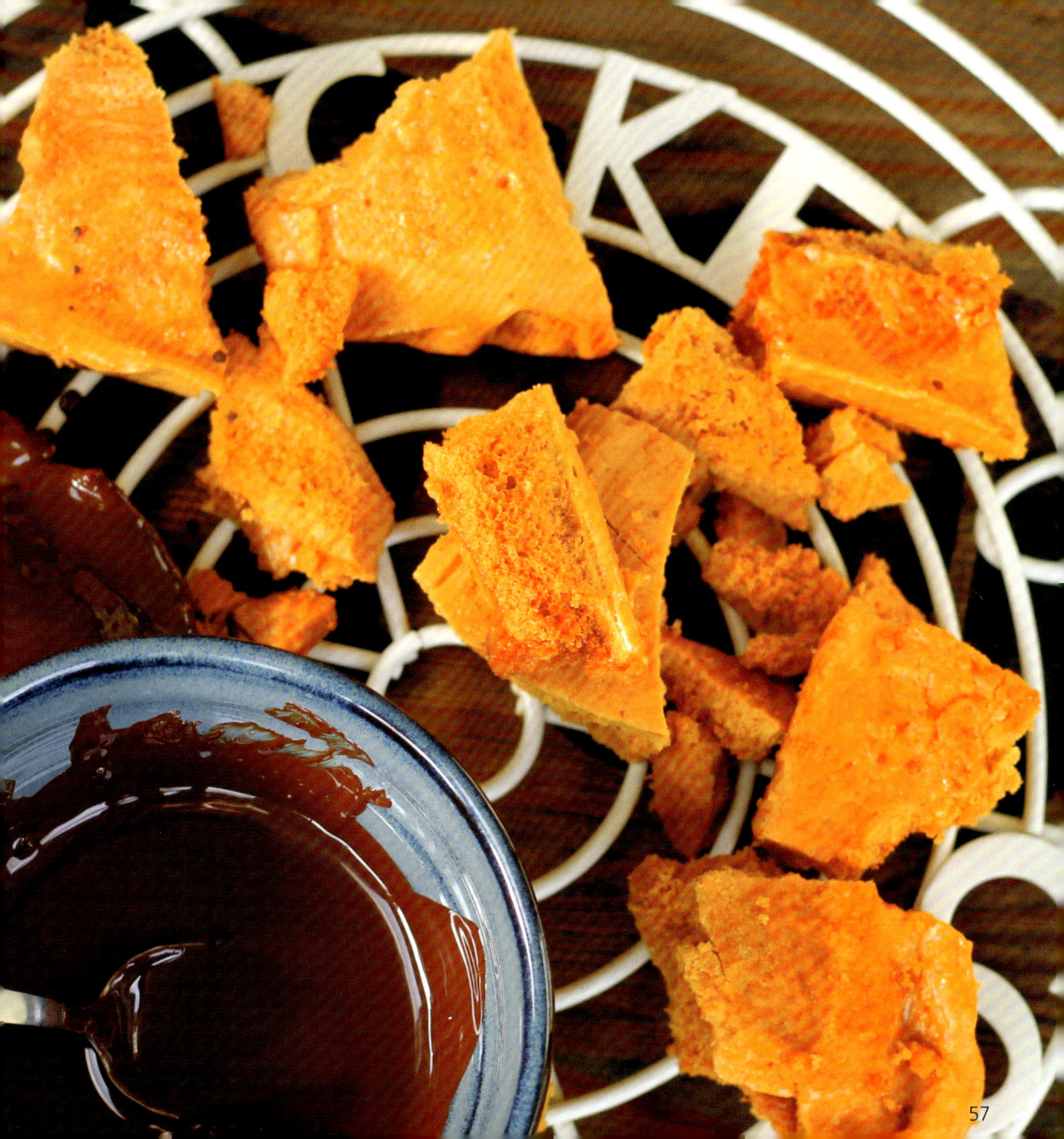

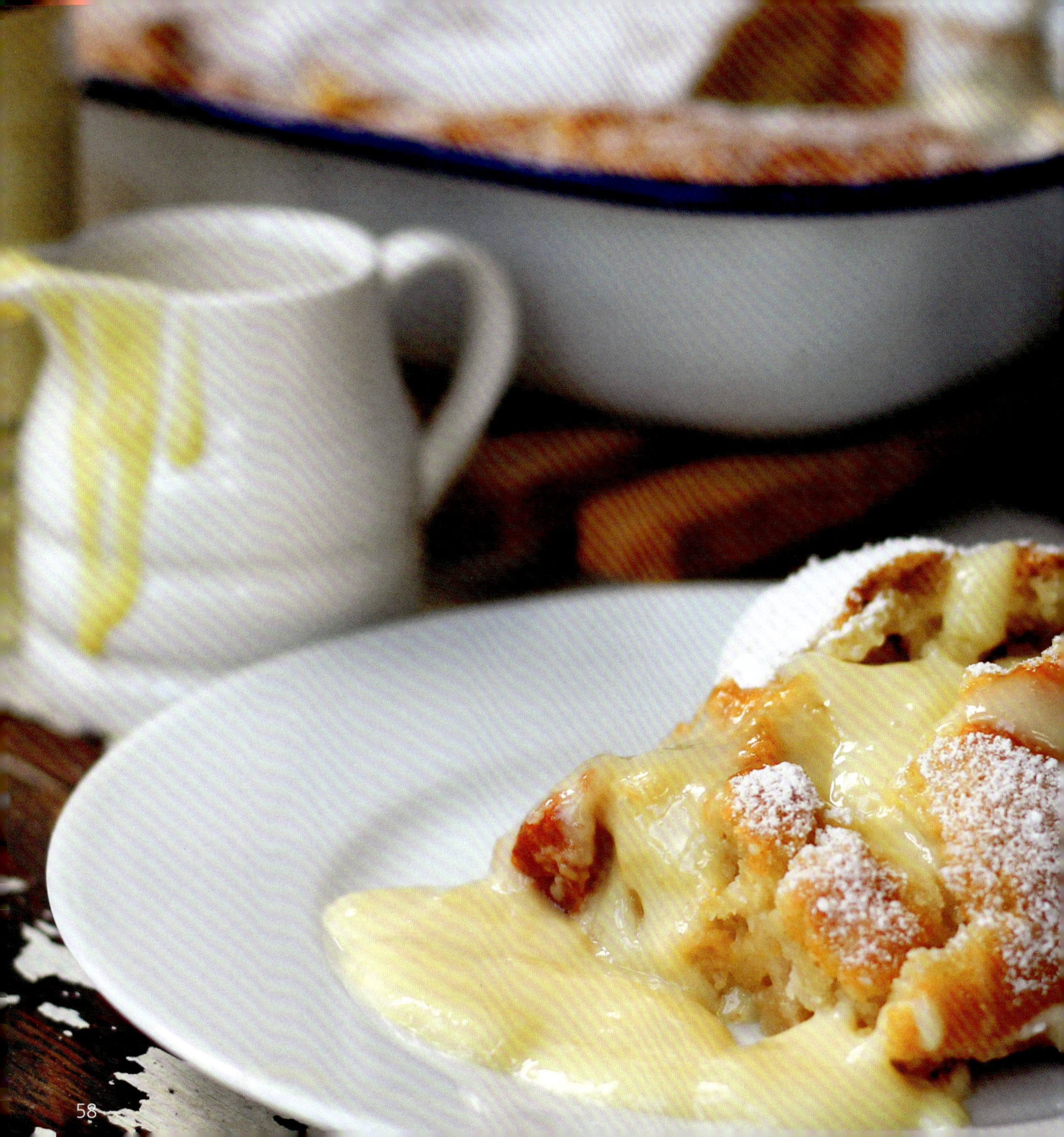

Eve's Apple Sponge Pudding

Serves 4-6 | 40 minutes
This is an old traditional pudding that we have veganised. It's deeply comforting and tasty.

Apple filling
- 2 large cooking apples – approximately 500g/a generous 1lb – peeled and thinly sliced
- 3 tbsp dark brown sugar (or any other sugar if you don't have brown!)

Vegan buttermilk
- 60ml/¼ cup plant milk, eg soya or almond
- 1½ tsp cider vinegar or white wine vinegar

Oil & lemon mixture
- 60ml/¼ cup plain vegetable oil
- 1½ tsp lemon essence
- 2 tbsp lemon juice

Sponge – dry ingredients
- 180g/1¼ cups plain white flour
- 1 tsp baking powder
- ¼ tsp bicarbonate of soda
- ¼ tsp salt
- 150g/¾ cup caster sugar
- Lemon zest

Aquafaba mixture
- 3 tbsp chickpea or other tinned white bean water

Serving options
- Vegan custard, vegan cream or vegan ice cream

1 Pre-heat the oven to 180°/350°F/Gas Mark 4.
2 Grease the baking tin or dish, layer the sliced apples in it, sprinkle the sugar over the slices and set aside.
3 Make the vegan buttermilk by whisking the vinegar into the plant milk. Set aside.
4 Measure the oil, lemon essence and lemon juice into another small bowl.
5 Sieve the dry ingredients into the large mixing bowl.
6 Whisk the aquafaba (bean water) in the third bowl for a minute, until it is white and frothy.
7 Make a hole in the dry mixture then mix in the buttermilk. Mix in the oil/lemon mixture.
8 Finally, add the whisked aquafaba and mix in thoroughly.
9 Spoon the batter over the apples and bake for 20-25 minutes or until the sponge is just about all cooked – the bit near the apples might be slightly uncooked and creamy but that's OK.
10 Serve hot, with vegan cream, custard or ice cream.

All kitted out
- 1 large mixing bowl and sieve • Cooking spoon
- 3 small bowls • Measuring cups or scales
- Measuring spoons • Small whisk • Spatula
- 20cm/8-inch square or round cake tin, non-stick or silicone OR an oven-proof dish of the same size

Millionaire's Shortbread with Salted Caramel Filling

Makes 1 20cm/8-inch square tray | 20-25 minutes plus chilling time

Despite being so decadent and delicious this is partly raw and contains no refined sugar. However, it is very high in fat.

Base
- 150g/1¼ cups raw cashew nuts – cashew pieces work fine and are cheaper than whole nuts
- 50g/½ cup porridge (rolled) oats
- 4 medjool dates, pitted
- 50g/¼ cup coconut oil

Filling
- 350g/2¼ cups medjool dates, pitted
- 125ml/½ cup unsweetened plant milk, eg almond, soya, hemp
- 25ml/just under 2 tbsp syrup: eg maple, agave, rice or barley malt
- 150ml/¾ cup coconut oil
- 1 tsp vanilla extract
- ½-1 tsp salt. Start with ½ tsp, taste and add more if necessary

Chocolate topping
- 150ml coconut oil
- 5 tbsp cocoa powder
- 2 tsp syrup (see above)

1 Prepare the cake tin according to ALL KITTED OUT.
2 Remove lid from the coconut oil and place jar in microwave for 30-60 seconds. When it has softened, measure it out. Alternatively, place jar in a pan of hot water, but add a metal spoon to jar to prevent glass cracking.
3 Make the base. Blitz nuts and oats to crumbs. Add dates and 50g melted oil and blend again. Spoon into the tin and smooth evenly with the spatula or back of the spoon. Chill in freezer if possible; if not, the fridge.
4 Make the filling. Add pitted dates, plant milk, syrup and 150g coconut oil to saucepan and bring to a simmer. Cook for 2-3 minutes until the dates are very soft then add salt and vanilla extract. Blend until smooth. Taste and add more salt if necessary. Spoon mixture smoothly and evenly, as stage 3. Place in freezer or fridge while you prepare topping. Wash out the saucepan quickly.
5 Make the topping. Add another 150g softened oil to the saucepan along with the cocoa and syrup. Heat gently and whisk to get rid of any lumps. Cool for 5-10 minutes then pour over salted caramel layer. Return it to fridge or freezer to set.
6 Using the freezer speeds up setting time but only do this for 20 minutes then transfer to fridge. If using fridge only, it will take 2-3 hours to set.
7 Cut into squares. It will keep in the fridge for about a week.

All kitted out
• Cake tin: 20cm/8-inch square. If it has a good non-stick layer, just oil it. If it is an old tin, line with crumpled baking paper. Alternatively, use a silicone tin placed on a baking tray • High speed blender
• Spatula • Measuring spoons • Scales or measuring cups • Microwave or pan of hot water, to melt coconut oil • Small saucepan and cooking spoon

MY VEGAN TOWN
VIVA! VEGAN DIRECTORY

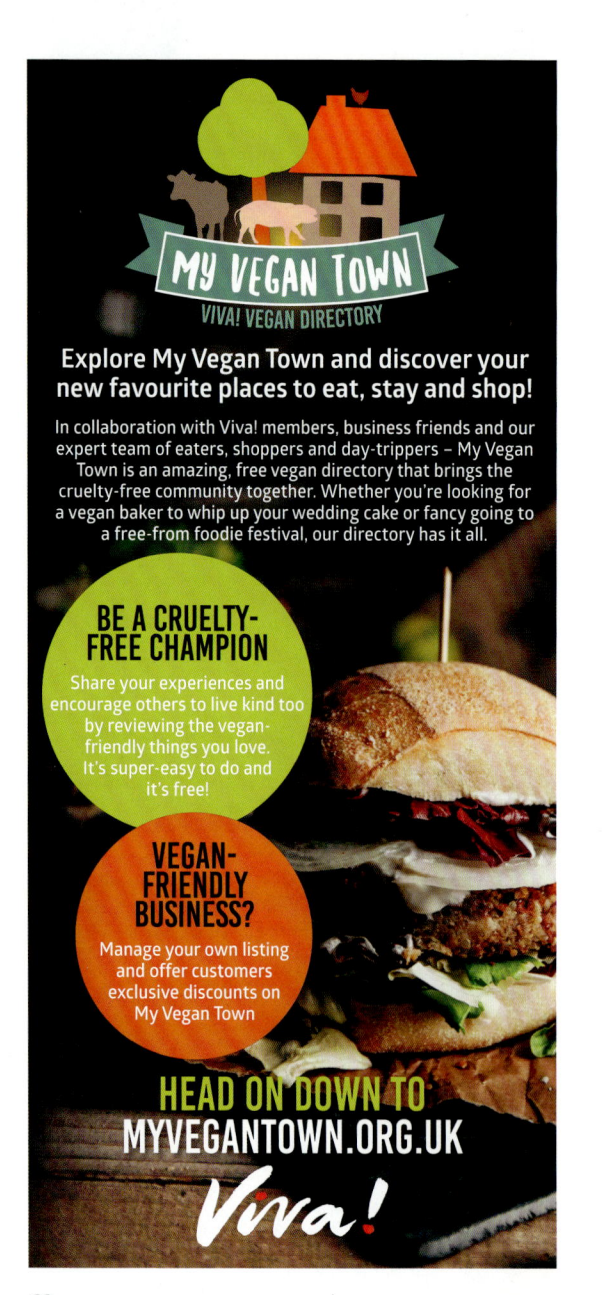

Explore My Vegan Town and discover your new favourite places to eat, stay and shop!

In collaboration with Viva! members, business friends and our expert team of eaters, shoppers and day-trippers – My Vegan Town is an amazing, free vegan directory that brings the cruelty-free community together. Whether you're looking for a vegan baker to whip up your wedding cake or fancy going to a free-from foodie festival, our directory has it all.

BE A CRUELTY-FREE CHAMPION
Share your experiences and encourage others to live kind too by reviewing the vegan-friendly things you love. It's super-easy to do and it's free!

VEGAN-FRIENDLY BUSINESS?
Manage your own listing and offer customers exclusive discounts on My Vegan Town

HEAD ON DOWN TO
MYVEGANTOWN.ORG.UK

Viva!

Vegan recipe club

- Inspiring, easy recipes
- 'Search by' facility
- Health advice
- Cookery videos
- 'How to' articles
- Cookery blogs

and it's *all* vegan!

VEGANRECIPECLUB.ORG.UK

Viva!